How to be a billionaire

Concise Edition

Tony Pow

Contents

Highlights 4
    Why you invest 4
    Why you want to read this book 5
    Introduction 7

Section I: How to be a billionaire 12
    Instructions on how to make a billion? 12
    1   Stage 1: Starting out 17
        Basic education / Simplest investing advice 17
    2   Stage 2: Find & evaluate stocks 18
    3   Stage 3: Invest in stocks for profit 19
    4   Stage 4: Protect your wealth 19
    5   For Retirees 20
    6   Billion-dollar ideas 23
    7   Billionaires' errors 25

Section II: Simple Techniques 30
    How to start 30
    1   Simplest market timing 31
    2   Quick analysis of ETFs 33
    An example 36
    3   Rotate four ETFs 37
    4   Simplest ways to evaluate stocks 39
    5   Simplest technical analysis 43
    6   The best strategy 44
    7   Don'ts for beginners 44
    8   Summary 45
    Bonus: Investing for 'lazy' folks 46
    Bonus: Sample portfolio 48

- Appendix 1 – All my books 50
  - Best stocks to buy for 2022 50
  - Sector Rotation: 21 Strategies 51
  - Shorting Stocks and ETFs 52
- Appendix 2 – Art of Investing 53
- Appendix 3 - Our window to the investing world 57
- Appendix 4 - ETFs / Mutual Funds 58

Highlights

Why you invest

You need to learn about investing sooner or later in your life. You need to take some calculated risks.

Compare the returns of the following assets: cash, CDs, treasury bills, bonds, real estate and stocks. We start with the risk-free investments and end with the riskiest. It turns out that the average returns are in the opposite order. Cash and CDs are not risk-free as inflation eats our profits. For example, the real return is negative for the 2% return in a CD and a 3% inflation rate. In addition you have to pay taxes for the 'returns'. <u>Our capitalist system punishes us for not taking risk</u>.

There are two kinds of risk: blind risk and calculated risk. If you buy a stock due to a recommendation from a commentator on TV or a tip, most likely you are taking a blind risk. It would be the same in buying a house without thoroughly evaluating the house and its neighborhood. When you buy stocks with a proven strategy (i.e. when/what stocks to buy and when/what stocks to sell), you are taking a calculated risk. In the long run, stocks with calculated and educated risks are profitable.

Be a turtle investor by investing in value stocks and holding for longer time periods (a year or more). "Buy and Monitor" is better an approach than "Buy and Hold" as some could lose all the stock values such as in the failure of Enron.

For experienced investors, shorting, short-term trading and covered calls would make you good profits. Simple market timing would reduce your losses during market down turns. If you buy a market ETF and use my simple market timing, you should have beaten the market by a wide margin from 2000 to 2019.

With so many frauds and poor management, do not trust anyone with your investing. Do not buy investing instruments that are highly marketed such as annuity and term insurance.

If you are a handyman and do not mind to satisfy the constant requests of your tenants, buy real estate in growing areas could be very profitable in the long run. Take advantage of the tax laws such as investing in a 401K especially the part that is matched by your company and/or a Roth IRA.

Why you want to read this book

This book should improve your financial health substantially. There are about a million investment books. Why we need another one?

- This is a lengthy book covering most topics in investing. Most of my paperbacks are eligible for a free digital version from Amazon.

- I select proven ideas from more than 100 books besides my original ideas and experiences. I also include links to current articles that will bring more depth to the topic. It is not a novel or documenting the story of my life. All related chapters are grouped in a section for easy future reference. Some chapters are not easy to digest as they have a lot of pointers and some may require you to try them out yourself.

- A best seller was written by a young writer whose main income was from his books and none from his investing. His book is good for beginners or you want to brush up your English. Most of my incomes are from investing.

- Many popular books claiming the authors making millions. However, usually their techniques are hard to follow. Many admitted they had been bankrupted many times. Hence, their chance of bankrupting again is very high. Is bankruptcy fine with you? I cannot afford bankruptcy past and present. My techniques minimize risking my money.

- There are many popular books. They worked very well at one time and folks making millions following the advice. However, look at their recent performances of the last five years. Most of them cannot even beat the S&P 500 index.

- Check the recent mediocre performance of gurus such as Buffett. They are the market and they cannot beat themselves. Their techniques may no longer work. Check out my success stories.
  http://tonyp4idea.blogspot.com/2015/09/successes.html

- The average performance of the hedge fund is terrible. You cannot depend on others to invest for you.

- One book describes ROE as the only theme (with the story of the life of the author to fill up the book). It is only one fundamental metric in my book. I modified P/E to include debt and cash for better predictability.

- **What to say** to your children why you did not buy him/her this book 30 years later. Colleges do not teach them how to achieve financial success but this book does. If you've achieved financial success after 30 years, do not thank me but thank the one who bought you this book.

My motivation to write this book

I would like to share my experiences, both good and bad. I use simple-to-follow techniques using the free (or low-cost) resources available to us. I have been successful in investing for decades. I am enjoying a comfortable financial life. I do not hold back my 'secrets' as my children are not interested in investing. It is my small legacy in sharing my investing ideas.

If you are looking how to make 100% return overnight, there are many other books claiming to do so and this book is not for you.

Market timing

The market timing works for the last two market plunges. It will work again in the next one as it depends on the falling stock prices. However, I hope it will give us the ample time to exit as the last two. This simple chart is the best-kept secret. I'm the one to publicize it and for doing that it makes a lot of folks angry with me. There is nothing to buy or subscribe as it is free from many websites.

It is better but not possible to sell at the top and buy at the bottom. I summarize these conditions in this book. After we've detected the market top conditions, use stops to protect our profits. I will describe a better way than stops to avoid flash crash.

The smart investor never sells at the peak as the peak is too risky.

Introduction

This is the concise version.

Most likely this book will not make you a billionaire. I'm not a billionaire. If I were one, do you think I have the time to write a book? It is used to catch your attention. The title "How to be a 10 millionaire" does not sound too appealing. When a child wants to be a president, most likely he or she will end up at least a good citizen. Aim high.

However, if you're young, 10 million (in 2020's money) is very doable. I separated this book into 4 stages on the road to become a "billionaire". If I had this book or a similar book when I started out, I could have made over 10 million by now. I hope my readers will.

When you are a recent college graduate, buy this book and start with Stage 1. It makes the ideal gift to a recent college graduate and s/he will thank you forever. It is truly a gift keeping on gifting. If you have the basic knowledge and time in investing, glance through Stage 1 and 2.

You do not learn from someone you do not respect. If some of my readers bought the 15 or so stocks mentioned in my article Amazing Returns, in a year they would have made more money than any other articles published in any investing site. Some asked me for proofs and some blamed me for high commission costs, etc. All these questions were due to no respect. The fact is it returned more than 50% in a year from the publish date and I claim to be the best performing article in a year for recommending more than 15 stocks in diversified sectors.

Stage 1

It is for young folks such as recent college graduates. Unless you are in investing industry, you do not want to spend a lot of time in investing. You have a life too! At this stage, concentrate in your career. Accumulate cash for an emergency fund to support you for six months and down payment for a house. Invest fully in Roth IRA (if you're eligible), at least the matched part of your 401K if available and ETFs for the extra fund.

Do not marry someone who spends money like no tomorrow. Contrary to the popular new belief, you should attend a good college even the monetary payback may not be good. You have a higher chance to find a compatible spouse with less chance of a divorce. A greasy lady graduated from a technical institute is not too appealing to me.

I design a simple plan on how to invest in ETFs and a simple way to time the market. It takes about 10 minutes on the first (or any) day of a month in investing.

Stage 2

Learn how to invest in the market. Use paper trade. I provide you all the tools. Depending on your time, learn stock investing but do not use real money. Knowledge means success. However, little and/or any misinterpretation could cost you money.

Stage 3

Invest in the market with real money. Start it small and increase your purchases gradually. It is the gut of this book covering most areas in profitable investing. The techniques are discussed in Advanced Topic Section. Stay away from day trading that this book does not describe; most newcomers lose money in day trading.

Stage 4

Protect your profits and donate some to the poor. In this stage, your health is more important than all the gold in the world.

Billionaires among us

Every generation has its opportunities to produce billionaires. In our generation, we have Bill Gates, Warren Buffett and many others. I prefer to set a 'modest' target of 10 million (in 2015's money) and be a turtle investor. Actually I know many folks with about a million dollars that are having a happy retirement. You do not need a billion to enjoy your retirement or have a happy life at least financially. Here is why:

Jesse Livermore, considered to be the greatest trader, made millions and bankrupted several times. Finally he committed suicide. It is better to be a turtle, boring investor. It is easy for the mind to make millions, but tough to lose millions. Examples abound.

I know two or three billionaires personally. They all have something in common: Participate in IPOs in Chinese companies. It is once-in-a-life-time opportunity to build bridges between the US and the Chinese businesses. It is similar to the Walton family making billions by importing Chinese products. What a simple idea and why did I miss it?

The objectives in life

We come to this earth with nothing and leave with nothing. Why do we fight for wealth, prestige and power? However, if we do not have the objective for wealth, prestige and power, it is a life without meaning at least for me.

Money should not be our primary objective in life and happiness and health have to be earned and cannot be bought with money. When you've accumulated enough wealth to have a comfortable financial life, you may want to pursue other objectives in life besides wealth.

I have seen many successful men and women who are not wealthy using financial yardsticks but they are wealthy in working in jobs they love, good friends, good families, good health and/or fulfilling their own objectives in life such as helping the poor.

Most likely when you've accumulated enough wealth for a financially secured life, there are many objectives in life more important than wealth such as happiness and health. Still not convinced? Check out the wealthy singers, movie stars and athletes. Are most of them really happy with all the broken marriages, drug and alcohol abuses...? I rest my case. Many of them do not have basic investing knowledge (most likely they have not read this book), and end up bankrupt.

I do not believe most authors on investing are rich. Unless they do it for fun, the successful ones do not want to reveal their secrets. As of this writing, I'm financially sound especially with my age and my frugal lifestyle. I do it for fun and I read my own books to remind me of my mistakes in investing. The best trader in our generation committed suicide losing all his money and called himself a loser.

Learn from his failure: 1. He did not practice what he preached and 2. Risky bets. My books preach about being a turtle investor.

One friend accused me of my greedy investing. Does he favor the 1% or the 40% who do not pay any Federal income tax?

He accused the 1% (I do not belong in this group) of altering the tax laws to reduce their taxes. It is partly true and Buffett should not pay less than the tax rate of his secretary. Many rich folks donate their wealth to charities. Without the 60%, where do we have money to subsidize the 40%?

We should encourage the 40% to work. The current system takes away their benefits for taking a job. I contribute by paying income taxes when I make money in the stock market. A good market allows me to help the poor. Investors buy stocks to finance new products and services and hence boost employment. Capitalism is not evil.

The six pillars of success

They are hard work, persistence, innovation, honesty, passion and social responsibility, in random order. Why is luck not one of them? Most successful folks do not attribute the success to luck.

Also successful folks also are humble in learning how and why others are successful. Successful folks do make mistakes but they try hard not to repeat their mistakes. They also learn from others' mistakes. Now, you are ready to set your objectives and enjoy your road to wealth.

Why you want to gift this book
What should you tell your children about why you did not buy him/her this book 30 years from now? Colleges do not teach them how to achieve financial success but this book does. If you've achieved financial success after 30 years, do not thank me but thank the one who bought you this book – Pat your shoulder if you bought this book for yourself.

Important notices
© 2021-2022 Tony Pow. Email ID: pow_tony@yahoo.com

Version	Paperback	Kindle
1.0	03/15	03/15

2.0	03/22	03/22

No part of this book can be reproduced in any form without the written approval of the author.

Book store managers can order this book from Createspace.com. https://tonyp4idea.blogspot.com/2020/12/book-managers.html

Book update.
https://ebmyth.blogspot.com/2020/12/updates-for-all-books.html

Disclaimer

Do not gamble with money that you cannot afford to lose. Past performance is a guideline and is not necessarily indicative of future results. All information is believed to be accurate, but there is not a guarantee. All the strategies including charts to detect market plunges described have no guarantee that they will make money and they may lose money. Do not trade without doing due diligence and be warned that most data may be obsolete. All my articles and the associated data are for informational and illustration purposes only. I'm not a professional investment counselor, a tax professional or any other field. Seek one before you make any investment decisions. Remember to consult with a registered financial adviser before making any investment decisions. The above mentioned also applies for all other advice such as on accounting, taxes, health and any topic mentioned in this book. Tax laws change all the time, so talk to your tax advisors before taking any action. Some articles may offend some one or some organization unintentionally. If I did, I'm sorry about that. I am politically and religiously neutral. I have provided my best efforts to ensure the accuracy of my articles. Data also from different sources was believed to be accurate. However, there is no guarantee that they are accurate and suitable for the current market conditions and /or your individual situations. The values of some parameters such as RSI(14) are arbitrarily set by me. My publisher and I are not liable for any damages in using this book or its contents.

How the rate of return is calculated

They are for education purposes only, and do not make your investing decisions based on them. I usually use annualized for better comparisons; 4% in a month is more than 5% in a year for example. For short-term strategies including momentum, shorting and year-end strategy, I use the returns for a month, and sometimes 2 months. For simplicity, most of my returns do not include commissions, exchange fees, order spread and dividends. The return = profit / investment. I am not and my publisher are not liable for any error.

Section I: How to be a billionaire

Instructions on how to make a billion?

Most likely this book will not make you a billionaire. I'm not one myself. If I were one, do you think I have the time to write a book? It is used to catch your attention. The title "How to be a 10 millionaire" does not sound too appealing. When a child wants to be a president, most likely he will end up at least a good citizen. Aim high.

However, if you're young, 10 million (in 2020's money) is very doable. I separated this book into 4 stages. If I had this book or a similar book when I started out, I could have made over 10 million by now.

When you become a recent college graduate, buy this book and start with Stage 1. They do not teach you how to become rich in college. It makes the ideal gift for a recent college graduate and they will thank you forever. It is truly a gift that keeps on gifting.

There are more important objectives in life than seeking wealth such as happiness, health, relationship, etc. With wealth, a wise man can make the other objectives easier to obtain, but an unwise man can do the opposite. When you lose a lot of money and you're still smiling, you're a winner; the winner knows it is a temporary setback.

My friend died worrying about losing most of his life savings in the stock market. Eventually the market returned, but he was dead already.

Most of my friends making at least 2 million are investors in stocks, real estate or both. First we should be thankful as there are fewer wars than our parents and grandparents. It is easy to accumulate 2 million to retire in my generation.

Too conservative investors seldomly will be multi-millionaires unless you have inheritances and/or successful businesses. Our capitalistic system punishes us for not taking risks. You need to invest in stocks, real estate, or a combination of both. Both have advantages and disadvantages. The advantages of the former are usually disadvantages of the later, and vice versa. Most should invest in stocks and own his/her own house.

Advantages of investing stocks:
- Contrary to popular belief, investors are not parasites. You invest in companies that have good products / services, and punish poor management.
- Spend less effort unless you are a day trader. Invest in value companies and review them once a year and more often for swing investors.
- We can still invest when we are old, as investing does not need laborious energy.
- Do not have the problems in managing rental properties such as receiving rents and responses to repair/maintenance problems.
- The cost is low. Many brokers have zero commission cost. Be careful of the high-cost of borrowing from your broker.

Advantages of investing real estate:
- Tax advantages in the U.S (consult your tax advisor).
- High chance of long-term appreciation if the area is in a good location.
- Usually no need to swap properties.

From my observation, real estate investors are more frugal and mentally happier than stock investors; they do not know how much they gain or loss via the on-line statements. Small real estate investors need to be a handy man.

Stage 1

Unless you work in the investing industry, you do not want to spend a lot of time in investing. You have a life too I hope! At this stage, concentrate on your career. Accumulate cash for an emergency fund to support you for at least three months and a down payment for a house. Invest fully in a Roth IRA (if you're eligible), at least the matched part of your 401K if it is available to you and then ETFs for funds left over.

Do not marry someone who likes to spend money like there is no tomorrow. Contrary to the current popular belief, you should attend a good college even the monetary payback may not be good initially. You have a higher chance to find a compatible spouse.

I have designed a simple plan on how to invest in ETFs and a simple way to time the market. It takes about 10 minutes to invest on the first (or any specific) day of each month.

Stage 2

Learn how to invest in the market. Begin with using paper trades. I provide you with all the tools. Depending on your time, learn stock investing, but do not use real money initially. Knowledge leads to success. However, little and/or any misinterpretation could cost you money.

Stage 3

Invest in the market with real money. Start in small ways and increase your positions gradually. It is the gut of this book covering most areas in profitable investing. Stay away from the risky day trading; most newcomers lose money in day trading. Even many experts in day trading have their huge losses periodically. Value investing with market timing and trailing stops is the turtle way to make money in the long run. There is no substitution.

Stage 4

Protect your profits and donate some to the poor. There are more topics covered here. You should be very wealthy at this stage, if you have followed the book. Do not take extra risk on risky stocks. This is the time to enjoy your fruits in life.

Billionaires among us

Every generation has its opportunities to produce billionaires. In our generation, we have Bill Gates, Warren Buffett and many others. I prefer to set a 'modest' target of 10 million (in 2020's money). Actually I know many folks with about a million dollars enjoying a happy retirement. You do not need a billion to enjoy your retirement or have a happy life at least financially. Here is why:

Jesse Livermore, considered to be the greatest trader, made millions and bankrupted several times. Finally he committed suicide. It is better to be a turtle, boring investor. It is easy for the mind to make millions, but tough to lose millions. Examples abound.

I know four billionaires personally. The first two have something in common: Participated in IPOs in Chinese companies. It is once-in-a-life-time opportunity to build bridges between the US and the Chinese businesses. It is similar to Walton family making billions by importing Chinese products. What a simple idea and why I missed it? The other one is my high school classmate making movies in Hong Kong. Another classmate worked in MIT's post-graduate program and became one of the earliest employees of a famous drug company in the U.S.

The objectives in life

We come to this earth with nothing and leave with nothing. Why do we fight for wealth, prestige and power? However, if we do not have the objective for wealth, prestige and power, it is a life without meaning for most.

Money should not be our primary objective in life and happiness and health have to be earned and cannot be bought with money. When you've accumulated enough wealth to have a comfortable financial life, you may want to pursue other objectives in life besides wealth.

I have seen many successful men and women who are not wealthy using financial yardsticks but they are wealthy in working in jobs they love, good friends, good families, good health and/or fulfilling their own objectives in life such as helping the poor.

Check out the wealthy singers, movie stars and athletes. Are most of them really happy with all the broken marriages, drug and alcohol abuses? I rest my case. Many of them do not have basic investing knowledge (most likely they have not bought this $10 book and lose millions), and many end up bankrupted.

I do not believe most authors on investing are rich. Unless they do it for fun, the successful ones do not want to reveal their secrets. As of this writing, I'm financially sound especially with my age and my frugal lifestyle. I do it for fun and I read my own books to remind me of my mistakes in investing. The best trader in our generation committed suicide losing all his money and called himself a loser. Learn from his failure: 1. He did not practice what he preached and 2. Risky bets.

One of my friends accused the 1% (I do not belong in this group) of altering the tax laws to reduce their taxes. It is partly true and Buffett should not pay less than the tax rate of his secretary. However, many rich folks donate their wealth to charities.

Unfortunately only 60% in this country pay Federal income tax. We should encourage the other 40% to work. The current system takes away their benefits for taking a job. I contribute by paying income taxes when I make money in the stock market. A good market allows me to help the poor more. Investors buy stocks to finance new products and services and hence boost employment. Capitalism is not evil.

The six pillars of success

They are hard work, persistency, innovation, honesty, passion and social responsibility, in random order. Why luck is not one? Most successful folks do not attribute the success to luck.

Also successful folks also are humble in learning how and why others are successful. Successful folks do make mistakes, but they try hard not to repeat their mistakes. They also learn from others' mistakes. Now, you are ready to set your objectives and enjoy your road to wealth.

Until you retire, you should spend most of your time / effort in your career / business and NOT in the stock market. The swing in your portfolio would tempt you spending too much time in investing and that's not profitable in the long run.

Why you want to gift this book
What should you tell your children about why you did not buy him/her this book 30 years from now? Colleges do not teach them how to achieve financial success but this book does. If you've achieved financial success after 30 years, do not thank me but thank the one who bought you this book. Pat your shoulder if you bought this book for yourself.

The book "How to be a billionaire" is a perfect gift for college graduates. My other investing book for beginners is "Investing for Beginners".

1   Stage 1: Starting out

Why invest?

This is the only way to make money for the average person. Our capitalistic system punishes us for not taking risks (i.e. investing). It is easy to confirm when you compare the average returns of stocks and CDs in the last 30 years.

This stage requires you to spend minimum time by timing the market in its simplest form and buying ETFs that do not require a lot of knowledge and time to evaluate stocks.

Basic education / Simplest investing advice

Read basic investment articles for beginners. Both Fidelity and AAII (both require being a client or a subscriber) have excellent articles. Refer to "How to Start" in Section I. After you have funds for down payment of a house and emergency fund, I recommend buying ETFs such as SPY. When the market is plunging, sell the ETFs to accumulate cash. Move back to ETFs when the market recovers. For more aggressive investors, buy contra ETFs such as SH when the market is plunging.

Why market timing

Before 2000, market timing was a waste of time. However after that, we have had two market plunges with the average loss of about 45%. It sounds harder to time the market than it actually is. We have a simple technique to detect market plunges and when to reenter the market. Our objective is reducing the loss to 25%. Before you start Stage 2, practice what you have learned. Buy an ETF such as SPY that simulates the market when the market is not plunging.

Links
1 %: https://www.youtube.com/watch?v=ds5LQXBKtQg

2   Stage 2: Find & evaluate stocks

My steps to trade stocks

1. Search for valued stocks (from the proven screens).
2. Evaluate the screened stocks by:
    a. Fundamental Analysis.
    b. Intangible Analysis.
    c. Qualitative Analysis.
    d. Technical Analysis.
3. Sell stocks.

As with everything in life, there is no guarantee that this book will always make you money. However, the chance of success will be substantially improved especially when you practice all the ideas presented in this book. Start with paper trading first in this stage.

Screens (used to search stocks) are better than others in certain market conditions. You should have several screens and keep track of their recent performances. I prefer value stocks especially for beginners.

Learn about investing and test out some of the basic concepts. This stage gives you a foundation to the next stage that will use real money in trading stocks.

Continue market timing and trading ETFs as described in Stage 1. You're not ready to compete with professionals in trading stocks, but trading ETFs with market timing is fine.

Beside stock research

In this stage, you should enjoy the better things in life such as owning your own house and taking nice vacations. A trip to Washington DC should not cost a lot, but it is fun, memorable and a great learning experience especially if you have children. Buying a fancy car is consumption, and buying a decent house is an investment. Stick with investments.

3   Stage 3: Invest in stocks for profit

This is the gut of this book. I introduce long-term swing trading (i.e. keeping the stocks more than 6 months) as the first strategy.

In addition to Market Timing, Technical Analysis and Trade are included in this stage. You may want to start with mutual funds and/or ETFs. However, about one third of them cannot beat the market after fees. Depending on the time available, you may want to move a portion of your investments into portfolios managed by yourself.

4   Stage 4: Protect your wealth

Jesse Livermore, the best trader I believe, lost most of his fortune and committed suicide. Professor Irvin Fisher, the father of Wall Street, did not predict the 1929 crash and lost a bundle including most of his own life savings. Recently, the legendary Kirk Kerkorian's wealth reportedly reduced his portfolio from $16 billion in 2008 to $3.3 billion in March 2013. Examples abound.

This Stage introduces the following strategies: Sector Rotation, Insider Trading and Dividend investing. We should monitor our trades. Why are they big winners or big losers? Learn from both and trade accordingly. The rest is investment advice.

If you need a financial advisor, try to use the paid-for service. There is no free lunch and try not to buy their over-inflated services. When they try to sell you an annuity, run as fast as you can towards the exit door. Most annuities are written by the providers for their benefits. Very few have low-maintenance fees. However, the annuities before the market crash in 2020 perform better than the market. Do not attend any free seminars with fancy meals. Remember if you are the only one to buy their services, you have to pay for the meals for all the attendees.

5   For Retirees

The following describes my own experiences and yet everyone's situation is quite different. Check the current tax laws and consult your tax professional on any related topic. Also check my Disclaimer in the Introduction section.

Will and estate planning

They will lure you to their presentations by giving you meals at expensive restaurants. If your estate is small (such as below the Federal exemption), a simple will signed by a notary public and the assignments of beneficiaries in your broker's accounts may be sufficient. Gifting at the maximum limit allowed by law is a common and easy way to pass your estate to your children before you die.

Check the estate tax requirements in your state. Some investors move to another state that has more favorable estate tax treatment or even some people give up their US citizenship.

Many people transfer their houses to their children to avoid long-term care expenses. Check how to do it right with a professional.

I had several 'free' meals before I settled for my lawyer. He put my house into a joint trust. He advised me to put my largest taxable account into a trust account.

Taxes

I am lucky (or unlucky in considering how much taxes I pay) to have a higher tax rate in retirement than my working years due to my good investment return so far. Hence, it would be better for me not to postpone taxes during my work years. At 70 ½, we are required to withdraw our retirement accounts (except Roth IRA under the current tax law). Before 70½, I had converted some Roll-over IRA (used to be 401K during work) into Roth IRA as allowed under the tax law then. I paid taxes but it could be less at 70 ½ and/or if I start to annualize my annuity. Again everyone's tax situation is different and the tax laws may change.

Market Timing

Concentrate more on conservative investments such as CDs, Treasury bonds, safe corporate bonds and diversified ETFs. Save your emergency fund for at least three months after your retirement income.

From 1970-2000, the average annualized return is about 10%. Market timing may not help at all. However, since 2000, we had two market plunges (2000 and 2007) with an average loss of about 45%. For simplicity, read the chapter on "Simple market timing" and "Rotate four ETFs". For more detailed description, check out the chapter on Market Timing which shows you how to detect market plunges. To summarize:

- Do not invest during a market plunge.
- Invest aggressively in the early recovery phase of a market cycle.
- Invest conservatively during other phases with stop losses.

Make your money last

You may never run out of money if you withdraw 4% of your total asset every year.

http://moneyover55.about.com/od/RetirementAccountWithdrawals/a/What-Is-The-4-Rule-In-Retirement.htm

Health

I highly recommend the book China Study by Dr. Campbell. In short, eat more whole grains, vegetables and fruits particularly with different colors and avoid meats / dairy products. Replace milk with soy milk. Avoid cakes, cookies and potato chips. Exercise regularly. Maintain both good physical health and mental health. This is a start on health and I am no expert.

Enjoy your retirement life with hobbies and travelling as long as you are healthy.

More information

This book concentrates on investing and it tries not to duplicate the financial topics for retirees from many well-written books. I obtained the following books in Kindle format for 99 cents each from Amazon.com.

Retirement Financial Planning for Baby Boomers by Whitney Smith.

Retirement Solutions: Financial Strategies for Today's Retirees by Michael Dallas, CFP. More related articles:

Retire overseas. http://www.marketwatch.com/story/5-reasons-not-to-retire-in-the-us-2014-08-07

Managed Accounts. http://blogs.marketwatch.com/encore/2014/08/05/managed-accounts-too-pricey-for-retirees/

#Filler: War-like or war-addicted

We have 16 years of peace out of 242-year history. The price is too big to be the big brother and the global police. Some wars such as Vietnam and Afghanistan were just wrong wars for us. This is the U.N.'s job, not ours. We have so many problems to fix at home such as homeless, drug / alcohol addictions, disaster control, shooting...

6   Billion-dollar ideas

Being good in your profession normally leads you to a rewarding life. Being good at investing would make you financially wealthy and that is what this book is about. Starting a business would make you very wealthy or make you very poor. The pandemic of 2020 bankrupts a lot of businesses.

Three out of four new businesses fail in the first few years. Jobs, Gates and Zuckerberg are good examples of success stories. However, they are the exceptions. After watching the Million Dollar Idea from the History Channel, I conclude:

- You need to have an innovative idea to start and it has not been used before.
- Every generation has its own opportunities. The three mentioned have their opportunities in the new PC. The internet has made a lot of billionaires.
- The clip-on lens inventor from the TV show has the opportunity of add-on to the successful iPhones. Clipping on others' success is not a bad idea, but it may not last long for profits without future products.
- Very few starters can afford advertising. Market share does not mean profit. Many advertisers of internet products in the Super Bowl 2000 went bankrupt.
- Investing with minimal cost such as at a trade show gains publicity.
- TV shows and magazines will knock on your door if your product is innovative. It will help them to attract viewers. It is free and effective advertising.
- Need to protect your product by patenting and keeping secrets during early development. You cannot save money in this area.
- Most inventors are not good businessmen. You want to let professionals run your business, but you have to keep an eagle eye on it.
- Be prepared to make a budget during early development, and plan to secure extra financing when the budget is exceeded – it usually does.
- Prepare for hard work.
- If your spouse does not join you in your venture, you have to choose between fulfilling your dream and keeping your spouse.

That's why so many successful entrepreneurs are single while starting their ventures.
- Prepare for failure and how/when to exit.
- Most new products have to go through many milestones before they become marketable products.
- Ensure your product is not a fad after its initial success. Follow-up products should be planned.
- Face the reality.

To illustrate, do not allow your bias on China to cover your eyes on business decisions. Many businessmen such as Walton and Apple contribute part of their successes to China. For some products, assemble them in South China as they already have component manufacturer's close by, cheap labor, fewer regulations and a large internal market. After the pandemic of 2020, it may change.

My own experiences

You may be thinking I'm giving advice from others' experiences. I did run a one-man company named Micro Architect selling software for over five years. My opportunity was that there was little or no software for the first (arguable) personal computer, the Tandy computer. What was driving me to work hard was my dream to think big and my passion was to make good money.

I wrote about 10 software programs. I spent money on two ads and gained a lot of publicity via press releases. I attended PC computer shows once a year in Boston. My wife's insurance covered the entire family. Larger companies have a team of more than 10 programmers developing a program compared to one person writing 10 programs. My exit strategy was looking for a full-time job when I found out my new programs did not sell well. I used a blanket to watch TV in the cold wintry days more than 10 years before they invented the blanket with sleeves. My friend thought about the won-ton making machines long before any such machine was available. If we only dream without actions, we will have to bring our regrets and ideas to our graves. Even if we fail, we will have no regrets.

Filler:
In any business, we can learn a lot from Bill Belichick. It is the same for stock research, we need to have knowledge, leave no stone unturned, work hard... Luck has nothing to do with success for most successful folks.

7 Billionaires' errors

Many millionaires (with assets over 10 M) I know have made fatal mistakes. Many should take good care of their health, enjoy their family and protect their wealth or forget their objectives in life. That's why most big lottery winners are not happy.

- With the millions, some eat and drink carelessly. Some do not exercise enough. Many die early.
- Many always work more than 100%. At least one person I know died early during playing tennis, so know your limits.
- Many 'smart' investors end up bankrupt. One more zero added to your net worth does not mean anything to them, but losing all will.
- Many famous singers and athletes die early or end up bankrupt. Many are drug addicts and some pass their problems on to the next generation.
- When it is time to retire, enjoy life and do not start a new business.

How I retired earlier
I retired in my 50s. My wife's insurance covered us for life. I am spending most of the time learning and testing investing strategies. Here are my comments with others on this topic.

- Do not borrow money and/or max out your credit cards except for the primary residence.
- Have an emergency fund up to at least lasting for 3 months.
- You do not need fancy stuff to make you happy.
- Invest in a weighted ETF for large companies such as SPY and spend a few minutes in market timing as described in this book.
- Invest your time and knowledge in maintaining good wealth.
- Marry your spouse with the same objective in your financial life.

Filler 12 noon is not 12 pm
The Chinese restaurant I went to says they are open at 12 am. Are they wrong or is the world wrong? The next hour after 11 am is 12 am, NOT 12 pm.

ETF	Normal	Today (2/2021)	Crashing[5]
SPY[1]	40%	30%	0%
QQQ[2]	5%	10%	0%
ARKK[2]	5%	0%	0%
VTIAX[3]	20%	5%	0%
LQD[3]	15%	20%	5%
GLD	5%	15%	15%
CD	5%	0%	0%
Cash	5%	20%	60%[6]
SH[4]	0%	0%	5%
PSQ[4]	0%	0%	15%

[1] VOO is a low-fee alternative for SPY.

[2] QQQ has more tech stocks, while ARKK is an actively managed ETF specializing in 'disruptive technologies'. During market crashes, avoid them, esp. ARKK.

[3] VTIAX is an ETF for global companies. LQD is an ETF for corporate bonds.

[4] SH and PSQ are contra ETF to SPY and QQQ. They are shorting the corresponding index. When the market is recovering, switch them back to SPY and QQQ.

[5] Need to balance the allocations about two times a year as ETFs can grow or shrink. When the market crashes, rebalance it right away. All markets will crash, and the last two (2000 and 2008) have an average loss of about 45%. Refer to the chapter "Simplest marketing timing".

[6] Today's low interest rate does not benefit us for CDs. I would leave the cash not invested and wait for the recovery to move back to stocks.

Of course, everyone's situation is different. If you are conservative, do not buy SH and PSQ. If you are afraid of inflation (especially due to the excessive printing of money), allocate more on GLD, a gold ETF.

Do not listen to financial news. They are used by institutional investors / analysts to manipulate the market. Many times they act the opposite from what they preach. This is the primary reason retail investors do not do better. With the GameStop incident, do not invest in most hedge funds. Buffett has proved the hedge funds with their high fees cannot buy an indexed ETF such as SPY.

The above is my recommendation. In the long run, it should work fine. Consult your financial advisor before taking actions. Most info is from RainIsHere, a Cantonese YouTuber.

#Filler: Simple measures to reduce net security.
Do not click any links from unknown sources. Some seem to be ok but not.
MalwareBytes, for checking viruses, is free for download (they do not pay me).

Personally, I use a Chromebook for my financial transactions and a two-factor login for my stock trading.

#Filler "How to make a 50% return"

https://www.youtube.com/watch?v=eEto5nEkf1Y

#Filler Buffett, the person.
https://www.youtube.com/watch?v=w-eX4sZi-Zs

ETF	Normal	Today (2/2021)	Crashing[5]
SPY[1]	40%	30%	0%
QQQ[2]	5%	10%	0%
ARKK[2]	5%	0%	0%
VTIAX[3]	20%	5%	0%
LQD[3]	15%	20%	5%
GLD	5%	15%	15%
CD	5%	0%	0%
Cash	5%	20%	60%[6]
SH[4]	0%	0%	5%
PSQ[4]	0%	0%	15%

[1] VOO is a low-fee alternative for SPY.

[2] QQQ has more tech stocks, while ARKK is an actively managed ETF specializing in 'disruptive technologies'. During market crashes, avoid them, esp. ARKK.

[3] VTIAX is an ETF for global companies. LQD is an ETF for corporate bonds.

[4] SH and PSQ are contra ETF to SPY and QQQ. They are shorting the corresponding index. When the market is recovering, switch them back to SPY and QQQ.

[5] Need to balance the allocations about two times a year as ETFs can grow or shrink. When the market crashes, rebalance it right away. All markets will crash, and the last two (2000 and 2008) have an average loss of about 45%. Refer to the chapter "Simplest marketing timing".

[6] Today's low interest rate does not benefit us for CDs. I would leave the cash not invested and wait for the recovery to move back to stocks.

Of course, everyone's situation is different. If you are conservative, do not buy SH and PSQ. If you are afraid of inflation (especially due to the excessive printing of money), allocate more on GLD, a gold ETF.

Do not listen to financial news. They are used by institutional investors / analysts to manipulate the market. Many times they act the opposite from what they preach. This is the primary reason retail investors do not do better. With the GameStop incident, do not invest in most hedge funds. Buffett has proved the hedge funds with their high fees cannot buy an indexed ETF such as SPY.

The above is my recommendation. In the long run, it should work fine. Consult your financial advisor before taking actions. Most info is from RainIsHere, a Cantonese YouTuber.

#Filler: Simple measures to reduce net security.
Do not click any links from unknown sources. Some seem to be ok but not.
MalwareBytes, for checking viruses, is free for download (they do not pay me).

Personally, I use a Chromebook for my financial transactions and a two-factor login for my stock trading.

#Filler "How to make a 50% return"

https://www.youtube.com/watch?v=eEto5nEkf1Y

#Filler Buffett, the person.
https://www.youtube.com/watch?v=w-eX4sZi-Zs

Section II: Simple Techniques

For starters, just trade ETFs such as SPY (an ETF simulating the market), and you can skip the rest of the book. It only takes a few minutes every month. When the market is not plunging, buy or keep SPY (or any ETF that stimulates the market); otherwise sell it. Do the opposite when the market is recovering.

If you have less than $50,000 to invest, just buy ETFs. Improve your investing skills by reading investment articles from this book and your broker's website. For example, Fidelity has a lot of information for investors.

Subscription to AAII is recommended. When your portfolio grows more than $50,000, invest on a subscription such as Value Line, GuruFocus, Zacks or IBD (more for momentum traders). Initially, use the information for paper trading on value stocks, which is usually available from brokers.

For the long term, knowledge is most important in your investing life and experience comes next. Retail investors have a lot of advantages over fund managers. However, I advise you NOT to be a trader. Hence, you should ignore the 'fabulous' trade systems that claim to be very profitable. Statistically most amateur traders lose money as they cannot compete with experienced, disciplined traders.

How to start

I recommend trading ETFs first and when the market is not risky. The very basic terms such as ETF are not fully explained here; try Investopedia for terms you need to know. Otherwise, this book would be doubled in size and it would bore most readers. Investopedia, your broker's website (especially Fidelity) and AAII (requiring subscription) provide many excellent articles. Alternatively, buy a book for beginners. Here are some freebies:

Click here for Morningstar classroom.
http://morningstar.com/cover/classroom.html
Click here for Vanguard.
https://investor.vanguard.com/investing/investor-education
Click here for Investopedia's Tutorials.
http://www.investopedia.com/university/
Click here for Yahoo!
http://finance.yahoo.com/education/begin_investing
Click here for Fidelity basic in investing.
https://www.fidelity.com/investment-guidance/investing-basics

1 Simplest market timing

Why market timing

Before 2000, market timing was a waste of time. However, after that, we have had two market plunges with the average loss of about 45%. It sounds harder to time the market than it actually is. We have a simple technique to detect market plunges and when to reenter the market. Our objective is reducing the loss to 25%.

Market timing depends on charts; the following describes how to use chart information without creating charts. Most charts will not identify the peaks and bottoms of the market as they depend on data (i.e., the stock prices). However, it would reduce further losses. It is simpler than it sounds. Just follow the procedure below.

The first part of this technique detects potential market plunges, and the second part advises you when to start reentering the market. It applies to individual stocks too. It also works to detect the trend of a sector (entering an ETF for the specific sector instead of SPY) and a specific stock.

How to detect market plunges without charts (similar to **Death Cross**)

1. Bring up Finviz.com.
2. Enter SPY (or any ETF that simulates the market) or RSP for equally weighed SPY.
3. If SMA-200% is positive, it indicates that the market plunge has not been detected and you can skip the following steps.
4. The market is plunging if SMA-50% is more negative than SMA-200%. To illustrate this condition, SMA-200% is -2% and SMA-50% is -5%.
5. Conservative investors should sell most stocks starting with the riskiest ones first such as the ones with negative earnings, high P/Es and/or high Debt/Equity. Obtain this info from Finviz.com by entering the symbol of the stock you own.
6. Aggressive investors should sell all stocks. Extremely aggressive investors should sell all stocks, buy contra ETFs, and even short stocks. I do not recommend beginners to be aggressive.

As of 2/12/2022, the following are from Finviz.com.

ETF	SMA-200	SMA-50	SMA-20	Death Cross?
SPY	-0.8%	-4.2%	-1.7%	Yes (Step #4)
RSP	-0.5%	-1.9%	0.4%	Yes (Step #4)

Both ETFs indicate the market is a confirmed crash from my indications using a technique similar to Death Cross. However, they are quite close, and we should keep an eye on these numbers. In this case, SMA-

20 has not been used. If it is a false alarm, golden cross would indicate it and you should return to equity; it could be quite common in volatile markets. The futures indicate that on Monday (2/14/22) the market would plunge further.

Another test is using SMA-350: When the current price is below SMA-300, it is a crash. SMA-20 has to be more negative than SMA-50 and it has not been used here.

When to return to the market (similar to Golden Cross)

Use the above in a reversed sense to detect whether the market has been recovering. However, when the SMA-200% turns positive, I would start buying value stocks (low P/E but the 'E' has to be positive, and/or low Debt/Equity).

1. Bring up Finviz.com.
2. Enter SPY (or any ETF that simulates the market).
3. If SMA-200% is negative, the market is not recovering, and you can skip the following steps.
4. Sell all contra ETFs and close all shorts if you have any.
5. Market recovery is confirmed when SMA-50% is more positive than SMA-200%. To illustrate this condition, SMA-200% is 2% and SMA-50% is 5%. Commit a large percent of cash (or all cash for aggressive investors) to stocks. If you do not know what to buy, buy SPY or an ETF that simulates the market.

How often to check the market timing indicators?

Do the above once a month. When the SPY price is closer to SMA actions percentage, perform the above once a week. The charts and data for market timing described in this book are based on SMA-350 (Simple Moving Average) that is more preferable than this simple procedure, but it requires some simple charting.

Nothing is perfect

If the market timing is perfect, there would be no poor folks. The major 'defects' are:
- It does not detect the peak / bottom as it depends on past data. However, it would save you a lot during the crash.
- It is hard to determine whether it is a correction or a crash.
- From 2000 to 2010, there was only one false signal. The indicator tells you to exit and then tells you to reenter the market shortly. In most cases, you do not lose a lot. After 2010, we have more false signals.
- The market may not be rational or may be influenced due to specific conditions such as excessive printing of USD. If you do not mind charting, use SMA 350 (or 400) using SPY. Buy when the price is above SMA-350 (or SMA-400), and sell otherwise. SMA-400 reduces the number of false signals, but it is not nimble.

2   Quick analysis of ETFs

Evaluate an ETF

ETFs are a basket of stocks according to the market, a specific sector, country or a specific theme.

Yahoo!Finance used to give the P/E of an ETF. Try to get it from ETFdb.com. Enter the symbol of the ETF such as XLU, and then select Valuation. If it is below 15 and above zero, it could be a value ETF. Also, if the current price is lower than its NAV, it is sold at a discount (or premium vice versa). Compare its YTD Return to SPY's.

Alternatively, get similar info from http://www.multpl.com/. In addition, this website provides the following metrics: Shiller P/E, Price/Sales, and Price/Book.

From Finviz.com, enter the ETF symbol. If SMA-20%, SMA-50% and SMA-200% are all positive, most likely the ETF is in an uptrend. To illustrate, SMA-200 is Simple Moving Average for the last 200 trading sessions (no trading on weekends and specific holidays). The percent is how much the stock price of the ETF is above the SMA. If the percent is negative, it means the stock price is below the SMA.

If your average holding period of your stocks is about 50 days, SMA-50% is more appropriate to you.

If RSI(14) > 65, it is probably oversold; if it is < 30, it is probably undersold (indicating value).

In addition, ensure the ETF's average volume is high (I suggest more than 10,000 shares), the market cap is more than 300 M, and it has low fees. Most popular ETFs have these characteristics. Beginners should avoid leveraged ETFs.

How to determine if the sector has been recovered

It is easier to profit by following the uptrend of an ETF using the above info. It is hard to detect when the bottom of an ETF has been reached. If SMA-20%, SMA-50% and SMA-200% are all positive, most likely the ETF is in an uptrend or it has recovered. It does not always happen as predicted, so use stops to protect your investment.

An example

First, determine whether the market is risky. Most beginners should not invest in a risky market. Advanced investors can bet against the market or a specific sector by buying contra ETFs or puts.

Next, you want to limit the number of sector ETFs by selecting those that are either in an uptrend or hitting bottom (bottom is hard to predict). Personally, I prefer sectors with long-term uptrends (indicated by articles found in many websites including cnnfn.com and Seeking Alpha.

For illustration purposes only for deteriorating market conditions, I would select the following ETFs: SPY (simulating the market based on large companies) and XLP (consumer staples). XLP should perform better than XLY (consumer discretionary) during a recession as those products are the necessities.

Technical indicators such as SMA-50 (Simple Moving Average for the last 50 sessions), SMA-200 and RSI(14) are obtained from Finviz.com and the rest are obtained from Yahoo!Finance.com. After you buy the ETF, use a stop loss to protect your investment. For example, biotech sector moved up for many months until it crashed in 2015. Change the stop loss value every month to protect your gains in this case.

As of 2/5/2016	SPY	XLP (staples)	XLY (discreet.)
Price	190	50	71
NAV	192	50	73
• Technical			
SMA-50	-4%	0%	-7%
SMA-200	-6%	2%	-7%
RSI(14)	44	50	36
Other	Double bottom at $186		
• Fundamental			
P/E	17	20	19
Yield	2.1%	2.5%	1.5%
YTD return	-5%	0.5%	-5%
Net asset	174 B	9 B	10 B

Explanation

- The figures may not be identical among websites due to the dates they are using.
- XLY has the best discount among the 3 ETFs as most investors believe a recession is coming.
- XLP has less down trend among the 3 ETFs as expected.
- XLY is more undersold among the three as expected.
- Double bottom is a technical pattern that indicates the stock would surge upward.
- SPY has a better value according to its P/E.
- XLY's dividend is the least among the three as they have more tech companies in the ETF. They have to plow back the profits to research and development.
- XLP has the best YTD return among the three.
- As long as the asset is above 500 M (200 M for specialized ETFs), it is fine and all three pass this mark.

There are many metrics such as Debt/Equity not readily available from most websites. Many sites list the top holdings of a specific ETF. Just average the metrics of the top ten or so of its stock holdings.

#Filler: Illogical logic

If we do not test for the pandemic, we would have zero increase in this pandemic. Some silly folks buy this argument. What happens to the once-great country?

Filler: The problems of the U.S.

1. Our political system. We waste time arguing between the two parties. There is no long-term planning, as the other party could claim the credit. Same as corporations' CEOs who care about their yearly bonuses.
2. The politicians have to satisfy their voters. Today give them free cash by jacking up the printing press. And ignore the long-term consequences.
3. We have to protect our workers, our environment... Hence, we cannot compete with many countries.
4. We have spent too much on the military and ignore our crumbling infrastructure.
5. Historically no country can rule the world forever.
6. We blame China, but ignore how hard-working Chinese are.

An example

This example evaluates RING, a gold miner, using ETFdb and Finviz that are free from the web. The data is from July, 6, 2020.

Bring up ETFdb and enter RING in the search. There is basic info that are important to me: Sector (gold miners), Asset Size (Large-Cap), Issuer (iShares), Inception (Jan. 31, 2012), Expense Ratio (0.39%) and Tax Form (1099).

They fit all my requirements. The expense ratio is higher than most ETFs that simulate an index such as SPY. I try to trade ETFs using Tax Form 1099 in my taxable accounts. The large cap created about 8 years ago by a reputable company is good.

Select "Dividend and Valuation". P/E of 17.39 is fine in a rank of 11 in 27 in a similar group of ETFs. As in my books, I stated it is hard to evaluate miners. I buy this ETF primarily to fight the possibility of inflation and the potential depreciation of USD. The dividend rate of 0.52% (0.70% from Finviz) is in the low range of the scale; it is fine for me as dividend is not my concern.

There is more info from this website. For simplicity, bring up Finviz:
- The short-term trend is up (SMA-20% = 8% and SMA-50% = 7%).
- The long-term trend is up (SMA-200% = 26%).
- It is close to overbought (RSI(14) = 64%; 65% to me is overbought).
- It is -4% from 52-w High. It has performed well from the YTD, Last Year, Last Quarter, Last Month and Last Week.
- It almost doubled in price from mid-March this year.
- Avg. Vol. is fine.

From ETFdb, check the Holding. It has 39 stocks, so it is quite diversified for this industry. The two top holdings are NEM (19%) and ABX (18%), which is listed as GOLD in NYSX. I also consider buying these two stocks in addition to RING. You can estimate the other metrics that are not available by averaging these two stocks. Here is my summary:

STOCK	NEM	GOLD
Forward P/E	20	25
Debt / Share	0.31	0.24
ROE	17%	22%
Sales Q/Q	43%	30%
EPS Q/Q	389%	254%
SMA50	2%	4%
RSI(14)	59%	60%
Insider Trans	-13%	N/A

| Fidelity's Equity Summary Score | 6.1 | 6.8 |

3 Rotate four ETFs

We can beat the market by rotating one ETF that represents the market such as SPY and cash via market timing. Aggressive investors can add SH or PSQ (contra ETFs) to the four to have better returns during market plunges.

During a market uptrend, rotating the following four ETFs could be more profitable than staying with SPY (or any ETF that simulates the market). Be warned that a short-term capital gain in taxable accounts is not treated as favorably as the long-term capital gain; check current tax laws.

The allocation percentages depend on your individual risk tolerance. You can use indexed mutual funds. Compare their expenses and restrictions. Some mutual funds charge you if you withdraw within a specific time period.

Select the best performer of last month (from Seeking Alpha, cnnFn, or one of many ETF/mutual fund sites). Add a contra ETF such as SH to take advantage of a falling market for more aggressive investors. Add sector ETFs to the described four ETFs such as XLY, XLP, XLE, XLF, XLU, IYW, XHB, IYM, OIL and XLU to expand your selection.

ETFs	Money Market	U.S.	International	Bond
Fidelity		Spartan Total Market	Spartan Global Market	Spartan US Bond
Vanguard		Total Stock Market	Total International Market	Total Bond Market
My choice	Fidelity	SPY	Vanguard	Fidelity
Suggest %				
During Market plunge	90%	0%	0%	10%
After plunge	10%	60%	20%	10%

Explanation

- The above are suggestions only. If your broker offers similar ETFs, consider using them.
- Check out any restrictions of the ETFs and commissions.
- 4 ETFs (one actually is a money market fund) are enough for most starters. They are diversified, low-cost and you do not need rebalancing except during a market plunge.
- The percentages are suggestions only. If you are less risk tolerant, allocate more to a money market fund, CD and/or bond ETF.
- Have at least 10% allocated to the money market fund for safety.
- When the market is risky, reduce stock equities (i.e., increase money market and bond allocations).
- The symbols for Fidelity ETFs are FSTMX, FSGDX and FBIDX.
- The symbols for Vanguard ETFs are VTSMX, VGTSX and VBMFX.
- If you are more advanced, use additional sector ETFs to rotate. Also buy long-term bond funds (such as 30-year Treasury) when the interest rate is 10% or more.

#Filler: Glad to be an investor

After watching the following YouTube video, I am glad my parents did not push me to play piano and also glad I do not have any musical gene. How can I compete with this kid?

https://www.youtube.com/watch?v=yf0B4rVoq44

Also, glad not into some life-threatening professions such as surgical doctors, soldiers, fire fighters, etc. I can make mistakes in investing from time to time without suffering from the consequences. With the uptrend market for most of the last 50 years, most investors should make good money. Thank God.

#Filler: Where common sense is not common sense

Excessive printing of money is not a long-term solution. Servicing the huge debt weakens our competitiveness. The politicians just want to buy votes today and finance their campaigns. Our next generations have to pay for these huge debts.

4   Simplest ways to evaluate stocks

Beginners should trade ETFs only. This chapter is for the readers who are ready or getting ready to trade stocks. In general, ETFs are diversified, less volatile than trading stocks. However, stocks offer higher profit but higher risk.

Many stock researches have already been done recently and some are available free of charge. I have no affiliation with Fidelity except I retired from it. You can open an account with them with no balance. Their Equity Summary Score is one of the best indicators; I check out **value** stocks with scores higher than 8. Concentrate on fundamental metrics such as P/E for long-term holds, and momentum metrics for short-term holds. Add criteria to limit the number of screened stocks. Finviz.com is a free screener.

Several sources

The popular ones are Morningstar, Value Line, The Street and Zacks (currently free for rankings of individual stocks). If they are not free, check out whether they are available from your local library. I have 3 simple ways to evaluate stocks starting with the simplest. In addition, read the articles on the selected stocks from Fidelity, Finviz, Seeking Alpha and many other sources for further evaluation.

Fidelity

Select only stocks that have Fidelity's Equity Summary Score 8 or higher. There are tons of information about a stock. Once in a while I did not agree with this score such as SHOP and ZM that scored high in August, 2020. Include the following for your analysis.

A modified stock selection based on a magazine article

Most metrics are available from Finviz except EV/EBITDA.

1. Forward P/E (expected earnings and not based on the last twelve months). It should range from 5 to 15 (10 to 25 for high tech stocks). EV/EBITDA (from Yahoo!Finance) is a better choice as it includes the debts and cash than P/E; it would be more effective if it uses forward earnings. If you do not use EV/EBITDA,

ensure Debt/Equity is less than 0.5 except for the debt-intensive industries.

2. ROE (Return of Equity) measures how well the company uses the capital. I prefer stocks with ROE greater than 5%.

3. Volatility. Conservative investors should select stocks with a beta of less than one (i.e., less volatile).

4. Insider Transactions for sales (i.e., negative) should be less than 5%. If it is -5%, most likely the insiders are dumping it.

5. Compare the metrics such as P/E and Debt/Equity to its five-year average and its competitors (available in Fidelity).

6. Momentum. Check out the SMA-50 (actually SMA-50%) and SMA-200. Ideally, they should be positive. SMA-50% is especially important for stocks you do not want to keep for a long time.

7. Check out articles on the stock as some recent events (for example a new lawsuit) have not been included in the metrics.

8. Compare the trend of the sector this stock is in. Under Finviz, enter the related sector ETF.

Summary

The sources are Fidelity (Equity Summary Score and various comparisons), Finviz and Yahoo!Finance (for EV/EBITDA). Value stocks should be held longer.

Category	Score / Metric	Value /Momentum
Score	Fidelity's Equity Summary Score	Both
Value	EV/EBITDA	Value
	P/E cheaper compared to 5-year avg.	Value
	P/E cheaper compared to its sector.	Value
	Insider Purchases	Both
Safety	Debt/Equity	Value

	Compare it to its sector.	Value
Momentum	50-SMA%	Momentum
	200-SMA% (for long term holds).	Value
Articles	Check out latest events	Both
Market	No purchase if market is risky.	Momentum

A simple scoring system using Finviz
Bring up Finviz.com and then enter the stock symbol.

No.	Metric	Good	Bad	Score
1	Forward P/E[1]	Between 2.5 and 12.5, Score = 2	> 50 or < 0, Score = -1	
2	P/ FCF[1]	< 12, Score = 1	>30 or < 0, Score = -1	
3	P/S[1]	< 0.8, Score = 1	< 0, Score = -1	
4	P/ B[1]	< 1, Score = 1	< 0, Score = -1	
	Compare quarter to quarter of last year			
5	Sales Q/Q	> 15%, Score = 1	< 0, Score = -1	
6	EPS Q/Q	> 20% , Score = 1	< 0, Score = -1	
			Grand Score	
	Stock Symbol Date[2]	Current Price	SPY	

Footnote

[1] Negative values for Sales (due to accounting adjustments), Equity and Book are possible but not likely.

[2] The last row is for your information only. SPY is used to measure whether it will beat the market by comparing the return of this stock to the return of SPY.

The Score
Score each metric and sum up all the scores giving the Grand Score. If the Grand Score is 3, the stock passes this scoring system. Even if it is a 2, it still deserves further analysis if you have time. You may want to add scores from other vendors. To illustrate on using

Fidelity, add 1 to the score if Fidelity's Equity Summary score is 8 or higher. Monitor the performance after every 6 months or so to see whether this scoring system beats the market.

Very basic advice for beginners
Beginners should stick with U.S. stocks with Market Cap greater than 800 M (million), Debt/Equity less than .25 (25%) except for debt-intensive industries such as utilities and airlines and Forward P/E between 5 to 20 (25 for high-tech companies). These metrics are all available from Finviz.com, which is free.

Do not have more than 20% of your portfolio in one stock (unless it is an ETF or mutual fund) and do not have more than 30% of your portfolio in one sector.

For more conservative investors, buy non-volatile stocks whose beta (available from Yahoo!Finance) is less than 1. Beta of 1 represents the market (the S&P 500 index). For example, a stock with beta 1.5 statistically fluctuates more than 50% of the market and hence it is very volatile.

Try paper trading to check out your strategy and your skill in trading stocks. If your broker does not provide one, use a spreadsheet to record your trades or check the availability of simulator.investopedia.com.

#Filler: Silence is golden

I am glad I did not give advice to a friend who had to decide whether to take a lump sum payment or an annuity. The correction in March, 2020 would wipe out a lot of his portfolio if he took the lump sum payment. No one would share his profits when the predictions are correct, but the blame if it does not materialize.

It is the same in investing that nothing is certain. With educated guesses, we should have more rights than wrongs especially in the long run.

5   Simplest technical analysis

When the stock, the sector that the stock is in and the market are all above its SMA-N averages (Single Moving Average for the last N sessions), most likely the stock is trending up.

1. Bring up Finviz.com from your browser.
2. Enter SPY. Write down the SMA-200 (Single Moving Average for 200 sessions). Positive numbers indicate that the trend for the market is up.

   However, the market could be peaking or overbought. Be careful when SMA-200 is over 5% and / or RSI(14) is over 65%. RSI is a metric on overbought / underbought.
3. Enter the sector ETF the stock is in. Write down the SMA-50. Positive numbers indicate that trend for the sector is up.

   However, the sector could be peaking or overbought. Be careful when the SMA-200 is over 10% and / or RSI(14) is over 65%.
4. Enter the stock symbol. If your average holding period of the stocks is 200, use SMA-200 and so on. I recommend SMA-200 for holding value stocks long term and SMA-50 for momentum stocks. Write down the SMA-N for your stock. Positive numbers indicate that the trend is up.

   However, the stock could be peaking or overbought. Be careful when the SMA-200 (or SMA-50) is over 25% and / or RSI(14) is over 65%.

If the above three criteria and the fundamental criteria are satisfied, most likely it is a good buy. If you buy sector ETFs or mutual funds only, you can skip step #4. In any case, use stop loss to protect your investment.

#Filler: The Ten Commandments of Investing.
http://www.investopedia.com/articles/basics/07/10commandments.asp

- Set goals. * Personal finances in order. * Ask questions. * Do not follow the herd. * Due diligence. * Be humble. * Be patient. * Be moderate. * No unnecessary churning. * Be safe. * Do not follow blindly.
- My additions: * Diversify. * Study market timing. * Protect your losses and profits. * Monitor your screens and your metrics. * Be emotionally detached from investments. * Learn from mistakes. * Stay away from bubbles. * Be socially responsible.

6 The best strategy

The best-kept secret in investing is to buy a weighed ETF. I use SPY as an example here. This ETF is well diversified as it keeps all 500 stocks in the S&P 500 index. The ETF has a higher position (in percentage) on stocks with higher market cap. The stocks with higher market caps usually grow the market cap by having good management and good products. The bad stocks are deleted from the index periodically.

The second best-kept secret is using simple market timing as described in this book to reduce the losses in market crashes.

It is very hard to beat this strategy. You do not need any knowledge in investing, and you only spend a few minutes every month to time the market. The market is risky when the metrics show you so such as the price is close to the simple moving average in using SMA-350 method; in this case you time the market more frequently.

7 Don'ts for beginners

- Do not use leverage: options, margin and leveraged ETFs.
- Do not short stocks.
- Buy low and sell high.
- Buy value stocks. Sell profitable stocks after a year and losers before holding 12 months for favorable tax treatments in non-retirement accounts. Be a turtle investor.
- Limit momentum trades.
- Use stops to protect your portfolio.
- Do not follow 'experts' blindly (most have their own agenda).
- Do not trade penny stocks (i.e., stocks less than 200 M and/or price less than $1 to my definitions).
- Venture into momentum trading when you have knowledge and time. Avoid trading systems that are available.
- Do not day trade. Most beginners lose most of their money.
- Do not take classes / seminars that promise you big money - if it works, they will give out their secrets.
- Be selective on investing subscriptions. If they give you a handful of stocks to thousands of subscribers, most likely the actual performance will not be good. Check their past performances that use real money.

8 Summary

The following improves the odds of success but there is no guarantee.

Risky Market?
Bring up Finviz.com. Enter SPY. If both SMA-50% and SMA-200% are both negative, do not invest especially when SMA-50% is more negative than SMA-200%.

Evaluate value stocks from others' researches
Gather a list of stocks from screens and/or recommendations from magazines. Use researches that are free. Value stocks should be kept for at least 6 months. In six months or so, evaluate the bought stocks again to see whether you want to sell the stocks. Some other sites may provide free trial or one-time evaluation: IBD, GuruFocus, Zacks and Morningstar. Fidelity requires an account but there is no minimum position.

Name	Pass Grade	Link
Fidelity's Equity Summary Score	>=8	
Value Line[2]	Timeliness > Average	
	Proj. 3-5 yr.% > 5%	
VectorVest[1]	VST > 1 and RV > 1	Link

1   Should be available from your local library.
2   Free for limited number of stocks and free trial.

Evaluate stocks
Bring up Finviz.com and enter the stock symbol.

Metric	Passing Grade
Forward P/E	Between 5 and 20 (25 for tech stocks)
P/FCF	< 15 and ratio is positive
Sales Q/Q	>10
EPS Q/Q	>15

Intangible Analysis
Bring up Finviz, Fidelity, Yahoo!Finance or Seeking Alpha (fewer articles now) and enter the stock symbol. To prevent manipulation, the stocks should have larger cap (> 200 M) and higher daily average volume (> 10,000 shares).

Bonus: Investing for 'lazy' folks

You have better things to do than investing or you do not have the time, the desire to learn and/or expertise in investing. You should be better off to buy ETFs.

I recommend the following 4 ETFs. If you have $100,000 to invest, buy $25,000 for each recommended ETF. Consult your financial advisor before taking any action. The recommended ETFs should have a large market cap (the ETFs themselves and not the stocks they hold) and have a high volume.

Most returns started on July 1 and ended on July 1 the following year; this article is written on July 20, 2021. All are annualized returns for easy comparison. Fees, commissions and dividends have not been included; you can add the dividend yield and prorate it for YTD return.

Symbol	Name	YTD[1] Return	1 Year[2]	5 Years[3]	Bear[4]
IWF	Russel 1000G	30%	34%	40%	-33%
QQQ	QQQ	30%	46%	42%	-31%
VTI	Vang. Viper Tot	34%	22%	42%	-35%
VUG	Vang. Growth	37%	33%	41%	-32%
Avg.		31%	34%	41%	-33%
SPY[5]		34%	21%	39%	-35%
Beat[6]		**-9%**	**60%**	**6%**	**7%**

[1] The start date is 1/4/2021 and the end date is 7/1/2021.
[2] The start date is 7/1/2020 and the end date is 7/1/2021.
[3] The start date is 7/1/2016 and the end date is 7/1/2021.
[4] The start date is 1/2/2008 and the end date is 4/1/2009. My estimates.
[5] SPY is the ETF for the S&P 500 index. It is used as a yardstick.
[6] = (Avg. – SPY) / SPY. Again, it does not include fees, commissions and dividends.

Comments:

- The YTD is the only period that this portfolio does not beat SPY (the market to many). It could mean the market could be changing the favorite from growth stocks to value stocks. However, 31% return is far above the average of the market.
- The one-year return beats the market by 60%.
- The 5-year return beats SPY only by 6%, but the return of 41% is nothing to sneeze at.
- All except Vanguard's Viper Total are ETFs for growth stocks. Hence, I expected it would not beat the market, but it still did by 7%.
- You can time the market using the techniques described in this book as often as you can. When the indicator tells you to exit, you can sell these ETFs and reenter the market when it recovers. Riskier investors can buy contra ETFs such as PSQ and SH instead of holding cash when the market is down.
- At least once in a year review the selection. Use ETFdb.com for information. If you do not have time, it is fine skipping the review. When you switch ETFs, taxes should be considered.
- Most ETFs replace some stocks periodically to ensure better appreciation potential.

Bonus: Sample portfolio

It is a suggested sample. You need to tailor it to fit your personal requirements and your risk tolerance. In general, you should have an emergency fund for at least 3 months (6 months preferred). Many of our generation have one or even no layoff. However, I estimate the current generation will have 3 layoffs in their work life. It is due to automation, artificial intelligence, global economy, etc.

The rough estimate of stock holding in distribution between stock and bond is equal to 100 – Your Age. To illustrate in the following three portfolios, I use a 30-year-old, and hence he should have 70% in stocks and 30% in bonds (including gold, CDs and cash).

In addition, some sectors are better than others according to the market conditions. The following three portfolios are for regular, todays' market and one during a market crash. I use low-cost ETFs exclusively. ETF is exchange-traded funds. They are traded similar to stocks, but most are more diversified; their fees are usually lower than mutual funds.

ETF	Normal	Today (2/2021)	Crashing[5]
SPY[1]	40%	30%	0%
QQQ[2]	5%	10%	0%
ARKK[2]	5%	0%	0%
VTIAX[3]	20%	5%	0%
LQD[3]	15%	20%	5%
GLD	5%	15%	15%
CD	5%	0%	0%
Cash	5%	20%	60%[6]
SH[4]	0%	0%	5%
PSQ[4]	0%	0%	15%

[1] VOO is a low-fee alternative for SPY.

[2] QQQ has more tech stocks, while ARKK is an actively managed ETF specializing in 'disruptive technologies'. During market crashes, avoid them, esp. ARKK.

[3] VTIAX is an ETF for global companies. LQD is an ETF for corporate bonds.

[4] SH and PSQ are contra ETF to SPY and QQQ. They are shorting the corresponding index. When the market is recovering, switch them back to SPY and QQQ.

[5] Need to balance the allocations about two times a year as ETFs can grow or shrink. When the market crashes, rebalance it right away. All markets will crash, and the last two (2000 and 2008) have an average loss of about 45%. Refer to the chapter "Simplest marketing timing".

[6] Today's low interest rate does not benefit us for CDs. I would leave the cash not invested and wait for the recovery to move back to stocks.

Of course, everyone's situation is different. If you are conservative, do not buy SH and PSQ. If you are afraid of inflation (especially due to the excessive printing of money), allocate more on GLD, a gold ETF.

Do not listen to financial news. They are used by institutional investors / analysts to manipulate the market. Many times they act the opposite from what they preach. This is the primary reason retail investors do not do better. With the GameStop incident, do not invest in most hedge funds. Buffett has proved the hedge funds with their high fees cannot buy an indexed ETF such as SPY.

The above is my recommendation. In the long run, it should work fine. Consult your financial advisor before taking actions. Most info is from RainIsHere, a Cantonese YouTuber.

#Filler: Simple measures to reduce net security.
Do not click any links from unknown sources. Some seem to be ok but not.
MalwareBytes, for checking viruses, is free for download (they do not pay me).

Personally, I use a Chromebook for my financial transactions and a two-factor login for my stock trading.

#Filler "How to make a 50% return"

https://www.youtube.com/watch?v=eEto5nEkf1Y

Appendix 1 - All my books

- Art of Investing (highly recommended combining most of my books on investing). It has over 500 pages (6*9), double the size of an average investing book. Similar books: Using Fidelity. Using Finviz.
- Sector Rotation: 21 Strategies and Shorting Stocks and ETFs have more specific chapters on the topic.
- Using Profitable Investing Sites. Investing Lessons.
- Best stocks for 2022.
- "Nuclear War with China?"
- Books for today's market: Profit from Coming Market Crash.
- The following books are in a series: Finding Profitable Stocks, Market Timing and Scoring Stocks.
- Books on strategies: Trading System, Swing (Rotation + Momentum), ETF Rotation for Couch Potatoes, Momentum, SuperStocks, Dividend, Penny & Micro Stock, and Retiree.
- Books for advance beginners: Be an expert (highly recommended), Introduce, Investing for Beginners, Beat Fund Managers, Profit via ETFs, Buffett, Ideas, Conservative and Top-Down.
- Miscellaneous: Investing Strategies. Buy Low and Sell High. Buy High and sell Higher. Buffettology. Technical Analysis. Trading Stocks.
- Concise Editions and Introduction Editions are available at very low prices and are competitive with books of similar sizes (50 pages) and prices ($3 range).

Most books have paperbacks. Links and offers are subject to change without notice.

Best stocks to buy for 2022

We care about performance only. Not considering dividends and fees, my last three books in this series have beaten the SPY (the market to most) by **110%, 71% and 25%** from the publish date to 07/01/2021. Next book could be on 12/15/2022

Book	Stocks	Return	Ann.	Beat SPY by
Best Book for 2021 2nd Edition	10	20%	52%	110%
Best Book for 2021	4	29%	52%	71%
Best Book to Buy from Aug, 2020	14	42%	45%	25%
Avg.	9	31%	50%	69%

Sector Rotation: 21 Strategies

- On 5/26/2020, I searched for "Sector Rotation" under Amazon's Book. They are listed in the same order except my book Sector Rotation: 21 Strategies.

Book	Date	Size[1]	Kindle $[1]	Hard $
Sector Rotation: 21 Strategies	**05/2020**	**425**	**$9.95**	**$24.95**
Super Sectors	09/2010	289	$26.39	$49.95
Dual Momentum Investing	11/2014	240	$40.40	$42.20
Sector Investing	05/1996	260		$29.94
Sector Trading Strategies	08/2007	164	$26.39	$16.66
The Sector Strategist	03/2012	225	$26.39	$44.96
ETF Rotation	10/2012	125	**$9.95**	$14.99
Optimal... Sector Rotation	07/2015	80		$44.07

[1] From Amazon on size and prices as of 5/25/2020.

My book won in all categories except the price for hard copy in one. However, my book won as the lowest cost per page by a wide margin. In addition, as of 5/2020 I bet that no author besides me made over 4 times using sector rotation starting the amount more than his yearly salary then.

- I have **21** strategies in sector rotation while most books have only one. It ranges from simple rotation of a stock ETF and cash for beginners to many advanced strategies for experts. Most other books have one or two strategies.
- Andrew, a contributor on Sector Rotation article at Seeking Alpha, said, "Great stuff, Tony. It's great to meet experienced traders such as yourself. I had a browse through the book and think your method is a little more refined than mine."
- "You have written the book in a way that makes good and logical sense." Bill.
- Do not be fooled by past performances. Just check the recent performance of the top 50 stocks selected by IBD in the last five years. The mediocre result (hopefully it will change) could be due to too many followers and/or there is no evergreen strategy. I seldom heard the fantastic results from the followers of O'Neil, our greatest chartist. The adaptive strategy of this book shows you how to select the most profitable strategy for the current market.

- I switched most (if not all) my sector funds in April, 2000 from technology sectors to traditional sectors (better to money market fund). We can reduce losses by spotting market plunges and the sector trend.

Shorting Stocks and ETFs

Recent performances.

Stocks	Short Date	Close date	Duration	Return	Annualized
ACVA	06/10/21	09/29/21	111	22%	72%
CCL	07/14/21	09/29/21	77	-8%	-36%
CENX	09/17/21	09/29/21	12	3%	105%
CLOV	09/16/21	09/29/21	13	10%	291%
CSPR	09/16/21	09/29/21	13	33%	917%
EOSE	09/15/21	09/29/21	14	10%	261%
MILE	07/22/21	09/29/21	69	53%	279%
NCLH	07/27/21	09/29/21	64	-5%	-27%
REAL	06/04/21	09/29/21	117	22%	68%
UAVS	06/04/21	09/29/21	117	41%	127%
Average	07/30/21	09/29/21	61	18%	206%
RSP	S&P 500			0%	

It is for education purposes and I am not responsible for any errors. As in most parts of this book, commissions, dividends and fees (interest for shorts) are not included, and hence the returns are less than specified. They are real and all trades for the period.

Stocks	Short Date	Close date	Duration	Return	Annualized
BBIG[1]	09/30/21	11/19/21[1]	50	35%	258%
BFLY	09/30/21	11/18/21	49	14%	107%
EOLS	11/10/21	11/17/21	7	10%	523%
FLDM	10/13/21	11/18/21	36	14%	147%
MKFG	10/27/21	11/18/21	22	-9%	-149%
PAVM[1]	10/20/21	11/19/21[1]	30	34%	413%
TSP	10/05/21	11/18/21	44	-11%	-91%
VRM	10/13/21	11/17/21	35	13%	135%
Average	10/14/21	11/18/21	34	13%	168%
RSP	S&P 500			4%	

Appendix 2 – Art of Investing

Art of Investing consisting of 15 books in 1. Besides saving money and your digital shelf space, it gives you quick reference and concentration on the topic you're currently interested in. It covers most investing topics in investing excluding speculative investing such as currency trading and day trading. It has over 500 pages (6*9), about the size of two investing books of average size.

The 15 books

Book No.	Amazon.com
1	Simple techniques
2	Finding Stocks
3	Evaluating Stocks
4	Scoring Stocks
5	Trading Stocks
6	Market Timing
7	Strategies
8	Sector Rotation
9	Insider Trading
10	Penny Stocks & Micro Cap
11	Momentum Investing
12	Dividend Investing
13	Technical Analysis
14	Investing Ideas
15	Buffettology

The book links are subject to change without notice.

"How to be a billionaire" is for beginners and couch potatoes, who can use the advanced features of this book in the simplest and less time-consuming techniques. Most advance users can skip this section unless they want to use some of the short cuts described.

We start with the basic books Finding Stocks, Evaluate Stocks, Trading Stocks and Market Timing. You can select and start with one of the many styles and strategies in investing such as swing trading and top-down strategy. Many tools are described in other books such as ETFs, technical analysis, covered calls and trading plan.

Many books start with "Why" to lure you to read more and are followed by "How" and then the theory behind the book.
If the book you're reading is beneficial to you, imagine how it would with 850 pages.

Most readers' comments are on "Debunk the Myths in Investing", which this book is originally based on. As of 2018, I did not know any of the commentators on my books.

"I skipped ahead to his chapter book 14 (of "Complete the Art of Investing"), Investment Advice just to get a feel of his writing style. His research is phenomenal and doesn't overwhelm with big words or catchy "sales-like" tactics.

I truly believe this ordinary man, Mr. Tony Pow, has a gift of explaining his experience as an investor without the bull crap of trying to make you buy his stuff. He seemingly just wants to share his knowledge, tips, and clarity of definitions for the kind of folks like me who want to understand something FIRST before jumping in with emotions of trying to make a boat load of money. I like the technical analysis side he brings.

Mr. Tony Pow talks about hidden gems in his book; well....quite frankly, he is a hidden gem. Thank you and I will also post my comments about this author to my Facebook page!" – JB on this book.

"Excellent book, recommend to all investors… great knowledge. It has fine-tuned my investing strategies… Your book is hard to set aside, as I read it all the time learning good techniques and analysis of stocks, ETF... Since I purchased your book in March, I have underlined, highlighted and placed tabs on top of pages for quick reference." – Aileron on this book.

"Tony, I just finished reading your 2nd edition. It's my pleasure to report that I found it most interesting. You're welcome to use this blurb if you like:

Debunk the Myths in Investing is an all-encompassing look at not only the most salient factors influencing markets and investors, but also a from-the-trenches look at many of the misconceptions and mistakes too many investors make. Reading this book may save not only time and aggravation but money as well!"

Joseph Shaefer, CEO, Stanford Wealth Management LLC.

"Tony, Great work!" from James and Chris, who are portfolio managers.

"'Debunk the Myths in Investing' is a comprehensive book on investing that deals with many aspects of this tense profession in which with a lot of knowledge and a bit of luck (or vice versa) one can greatly benefit...

Therefore 'Debunk the Myths in Investing' is an interesting book that on its 500 pages offer a lot of knowledge related to investing world and many practical advice, so I can recommend its reading if you're interested in this topic."
- Denis Vukosav, Top 500 Reviewers at Amazon.com.

"490 pages (Debunk) of a genius's ranting and hypothesis with various theories throughout, written light-heartedly with ample doses of humor...Yes, the myth of not being able to profitably time the market is BUSTED...

One might ask... Why is he giving away the results of his hard-earned research for only $20? He states that his children are not interested in investing and wants to share his efforts with the world." - Abe Agoda.

"Excellent book, recommend to all investors... great knowledge. It has fine-tuned my investing strategies... Your book is hard to set aside, as I read it all the time learning good techniques and analysis of stocks, ETF... Since I purchased your book in March, I have underlined, highlighted and placed tabs on top of pages for quick reference." - Aileron on this book.

"Great stuff, Tony. It's great to meet experienced traders such as yourself. I had a browse through the book and think your method is a little more refined than mine."

"Your strategy is very rules based and solid. I sometimes envy people who have developed something like this."

Making 50% in one month

I claim to have the best one-month performance ever for recommending 8 or more stocks without using options and leverage. My following return is 57% in a month or 621% annualized. They are slightly different as I calculated the average from the averages of three different accounts. The average buy date is 12/26/18 and the "current date" is 01/28/19.

The performance may not be repeated. I will use the same screen for the coming years and even the expected 10% (or 120% annualized) is very good.

I used the same screen for searching stock candidates. I spent a total of about 20 hours from Dec. 15, 2018 to Jan. 5, 2019.

Stock	Buy Price	Sold or Current Price	Buy date	Sold or Current date	Profit %	Profit % Ann.	Status
CHK	2.13	2.99	01/03/09	01/18/19	40%	982%	Sold
MNK	16.41	21.45	01/03/19	01/25/19	31%	510%	Sold
MNK	16.43	21.45	01/03/19	01/25/19	31%	507%	Sold
NNBR	5.68	8.58	12/26/18	01/28/19	51%	565%	
NNBR	5.72	8.58	12/26/18	01/28/19	66%	727%	
ESTE	4.35	6.45	12/26/18	01/18/19	48%	766%	Sold
LCI	4.61	8.29	12/21/18	01/28/19	80%	767%	
MDR	8.01	9.13	01/08/19	01/28/19	14%	255%	
YRCW	3.29	5.78	12/21/18	01/28/19	76%	727%	
YRCW	3.26	5.78	12/21/18	01/28/19	77%	742%	
ASRT	3.56	4.18	12/26/18	01/28/19	17%	193%	
UTCC	7.13	11.00	12/26/18	01/28/19	54%	600%	
YRCW	2.92	5.78	12/26/18	01/28/19	98%	1083%	

Best one-year return

I claim to have the best-performed article in Seeking Alpha history, an investing site, for recommending 15 or more stocks in one year after the publish date without using options and leverage.

https://seekingalpha.com/article/1095671-amazing-returns-velti-alcatel-lucent-alpha-natural-resources

Your choice for your next book

I was surprised that one told me $25 is a lot for an investing book. It could be less than a taxi cab to the airport attending a seminar, and the time is peanut comparatively.

"Investing Lessons: Successes and Plunders" and "Art of investing 2nd Edition" should be your first choices. If you are short-term trading, I recommend "Sector Rotation: 21 Strategies" and "Shorting Stocks /ETFs 2nd Edition". These books together with "Using Fidelity" and "Using Finviz" share many articles.

A new book every Dec. 15 with a July update (not a promise) is my selections on stocks. So far, the returns of the selected stocks are phenomenal. "A nuclear war with China?" is my views on politics.

Appendix 3 - Our window to the investing world

The paperback version of this chapter can be found in the following link.
http://ebmyth.blogspot.com/2013/11/web-sites.html

- **General**
  Wikipedia / Investopedia /Yahoo!Finance / MarketWatch / Cnnfn / Morningstar /CNBC / Bloomberg / WSJ / Barron's / Motley Fool / TheStreet
- **Evaluate stocks**
  Finviz / SeekingAlpha / MSN Money / Zacks / Daily Finance / ADR / Fidelity / Earnings Impact / OpenInsider / NYSE / NASDAQ / SEC / SEC for 10K and 10Q (quarterly) reports required to file for listed stocks in major exchanges.
- **Charts**
  BigCharts / FreeStockCharts / StockCharts /
- **Screens**
  Yahoo!Finance / Finviz / CNBC / Morningstar /
- **Besides stocks**
  123Jump / Hoover's Online / FINRA Bond Market Data / REIT / Commodity Futures / Option Industry
- **Vendors**

AAII / Zacks / IBD / GuruFocus / VectorVest / Fidelity / Interactive Brokers / Merrill Lynch /
- **Economy.**
  Econday / EcoconStats / Federal Reserve / Economist /
- **Misc.**
  Dow Jones Indices / Russell / Wilshire /
  IRS / Wikinvest / ETF Database / ETF Trends /
  Nolo (estate planning) / AARP /

Appendix 4 - ETFs / Mutual Funds

What is an ETF

ETFs have basic differences from mutual funds: 1. Lower management expenses, 2. Trade ETFs same as stocks, and 3. Usually more diversified but not more selective than the related mutual funds such as NOBL vs FRDPX.

The major classifications of ETFs are 1. Simulating an index such as SPY, QQQ and DIA, 2. Simulating a sector such as XLE and SOXX, 3. Simulating an asset class such as GLD and SLV, 4. Simulating a country or a group of countries such as EWC and FXI, 5. Managed by a manager(s) such as ARKK, 6. Betting a market or sector to go down such as SH and PSQ, and 7. Leveraged (not recommended for beginners).

Fidelity: Index ETFs (https://www.fidelity.com/etfs/overview).
Wikipedia on ETF (http://en.wikipedia.org/wiki/Exchange-traded_fund).

List of ETFs
ETF database (Recommended): http://etfdb.com/
ETF Bloomberg: http://www.bloomberg.com/markets/etfs/
ETF Trends: http://www.etftrends.com/
A list of ETFs. Seeking Alpha.
http://etf.stock-encyclopedia.com/category/)
A list of contra ETFs (or bear ETFs)
http://www.tradermike.net/inverse-short-etfs-bearish-etf-funds/
Misc.: ETFGuide, ETFReplay
Fidelity low-cost index funds:
https://www.youtube.com/watch?v=zpKi4_IJvlY

Fidelity Annuity funds with performance data.
http://fundresearch.fidelity.com/annuities/category-performance-annual-total-returns-quarterly/FPRAI?refann=005

Other resources
Most subscription services offer research on ETFs. IBD has a strategy dedicated to ETFs and so does AAII to name a couple.

Seeking Alpha has extensive resources for ETF including an ETF screener and investing ideas. So is ETFdb.

Not all ETFs are created equal

Check their performances and their expenses.

When to use or not to use ETFs

I prefer sector mutual funds in some industries, as they have many bad stocks such as drug industry, banks, miners and insurers. Most mutual funds cannot time the market.

When you believe a sector is heading up (or contra ETF for heading down), but you do not have time to do research on specific stocks, buy an ETF for the sector; it is same for the market.

Half ETF

Taking out half of the stocks that score below the average in an index ETF could beat the same full ETF itself. I call it HETF (half the ETF). You heard it here first. To illustrate, sort the expected P/E (not including stocks with negative earnings) in ascending order and only include the stocks on the first half. Add more fundamental metrics. It will take a few minutes.

Disadvantages of ETFs

- When you have two stocks in a sector ETF one good one and one bad one, the ETF treats them the same. Stock pickers would buy the one that has a better appreciation potential.
- Sometimes the return could be misleading due to stock rotation. To illustrate this, on August 29, 2012, SHLD was replaced by LYB in a sector fund. SHLD was down by 4% and LYB was up by 4%

primarily due to the switch. Unless you sell and buy at the right time (which is impossible), your return would not match the ETF's returns due to the replacement.
- Ensure the performance matches the corresponding index; it is hard due to excluding dividends.

Advantages of ETFs

- We have demonstrated that you can beat the market by using market timing. Between 2000 and Nov., 2013, you only exit and reenter the market 3 times and the result is astonishing.
- It is easy to rotate a sector vs. buying/selling all of the stocks in this sector. Rotating a sector is the same as trading a stock.
- The risk is spread out, and your portfolio is diversified especially for a market ETF or buying three or more ETFs in different sectors.
- Periodically the bad stocks in most funds are replaced by better stocks.
- Eliminate the time in researching stocks.

Leveraged ETFs

I do not recommend them. Some are 2x, 3x and even higher. They're too risky for beginners. However, when you are very sure or your tested strategy has very low drawdown, you may want to use them to improve performance. Most leveraged ETFs and contra ETFs have higher fees.

My basic ETF tables

I include some contra ETFs, mutual funds and Fidelity's annuity. Some of these may be interesting to you.

ETFs and funds come and go. Some ideas and classifications are my own interpretation. Refer to ETFdb for updated information. Not responsible for any error. Check out the ETF or fund before you take any action.

Table by market cap:

Category	ETF	Mutual Funds	Fidelity's Annuity	Contra ETF	Alternate
Size:					

Large Cap	DIA	See Blend		DOG	
	SPY			SH	FXAIX VOO
	QQQ			PSQ	FNCMX
	RYH				
Blend	IWD	BEQGX			
Growth	SPYG	FBGRX			FSPGX
Value	SPYV	DOGGX			FLCOX
Dividend	NOBL	FRDPX			
	VYM				
Mid Cap			FNBSC	MYY	
Blend	MDY	VSEQX			
Growth		STDIX			
		BPTRX			
Value		FSMVX			
Small Cap			FPRGC	SBB	FSSNX
Blend	IWM	HDPSX			
Growth		PRDSX			FECGX
Value		SKSEX			FISVX
Micro	IWC				
Multi					
Blend		VDEOX			
Growth		VHCOX			
Value		TCLCX			
Total					FSKAX
Bond					
Long Term (20)	VLV	BTTTX		TBF	
Mid Term (7 – 10)	VCIT	FSTGX			
Short Term (1 – 3 yrs.)	VCSH	THOPX			
Total	BOND	PONDX			
Corp Invest Grade	VCIT	NTHEX			
High Yield (junk)	PHB	SPHIX			
Muni	MUB	Check state			
Special situation					
Buy back	PKW				

Table by sectors:

Sector	ETF	Mutual Funds	Fidelity's Annuity
Banking[1]		FSRBK	
Regional	IAT		
Bio Tech	IBB	FBIOX	
	XBI	Large	
Consumer Dis.	XLY	FSCPX	FVHAC
Consumer Staple	XLP	FDFAX	FCSAC
Finance	KIE	FIDSX	FONNC
	IYF		
Energy	XLE	FSENX	FJLLC
Energy Service		FSESX	
Gold	GLD	FSAGX	
Gold Miner	GDX	VGPMX	
Health Care	IYH	FSPHX	FPDRC
	VHT	VGHCX	
House Builder	ITB	FSHOX	
	ITB	Perform	
Industrial	IYJ	FCYIX	FBALC
Material	VAW	FSDPX	
	IYM		
Oil	USO		
Oil Service	OIH	FSESX	
Oil Exploration	XOP		
Real Estate	VNQ	FRIFX	FFWLC
REIT	VNQ		
Retail	RTH	FSRPX	
	XRT		
Regional bank	KRE	FSRBX	
Semi Conduct	SMH		
Software	XSW	FSCSX	
	IGV		
Technology	XLK	FSPTX	FYENC
	FDN	FBSOX	
		ROGSX	
Telecomm.	VOX	FSTCX	FVTAC
Transport	XTN		

	IYT		
Utilities	XLU	FSUTX	FKMSC
Wireless		FWRLX	

Footnote. [1] Also check Finance.

Table by countries outside the USA:

Country	ETF	Mutual Funds	Fidelity's Annuity	Alternate
Australia	EWA			
Brazil	EWZ			
Canada	EWC	FICDX		
China	FXI	FHKCX		
EAFE	EFA			
Emerging	VWO	FEMEX	FEMAC	FPADX
Europe	VGK	FIEUX		
Global	KXI	PGVFX		
Greece	GREK			
India	INDY	MINDX		
Indonesia	EIDO			
Latin America	ILF	FLATX		
Nordic		FNORX		
Hong Kong	EWH			
Japan	EWJ	FJPNX		
S. Africa	EZA			
S. Korea	EWY	MAKOX		
Singapore	EWS			
Taiwan	EWT			
	TUR			
United Kingdom	EWU			
Foreign:				
Combination				
Intern. Div.	IDV			FTIHX
Small Cap	SCZ			
Value	EFV			
Europe	VGK			

#Filler: Honey, my book can play music.
https://www.youtube.com/watch?v=HxGT5z6d-GA&list=PLMZa6mP7jZ2b1otqG4tfbgZpLEdh6YiNF

It may cut down commercials by casting it to TV.